Immigrant Daughter

Temitayo Adewuyi

BookLeaf Publishing

Presentation by *BookLeaf Publishing*

Web: www.bookleafpub.com

E-mail: info@bookleafpub.com

ISBN: 9789357212151

First edition 2023

DEDICATION

To my family, my everything.

ACKNOWLEDGEMENT

I would like to express my earnest gratitude to BookLeaf Publishing, for providing me with the opportunity to share an original craft of my own with the world. They have given me the platform to create a novel that speaks to not only my experiences, but of many around the world. Additionally, I owe thanks to my mother, my greatest supporter, and undoubtedly the wind behind my sails. Under her encouragement, my passion for writing flourished and led me to the making of this novel. Lastly, I want to thank my friend, Prabhroop Thind, for pushing me to publish this book and to take a gamble on myself.

PREFACE

I wrote this book to make peace with my own experience with immigration and for children who have always felt divided growing up outside of their culture. Originally, I had no intention of executing the idea for this novel, but luckily the support from family and friends kept me going. Immigrant Daugthter speaks to real experiences and perspectives, not only to immigrants but to those who are the products of immigration. It is an homage to those who have had the courage to do what others can't; leaving everything that they know.

Oldest Daughter

The oldest daughter stands tall,
Speaks when she needs to,
And rigorously looks after everyone,
But herself.

Mama

The idea of a mother,
Has been sewed into our minds for generations.
She is kind, loving and caring,
And older.
But what was unexpected,
Was for the teenage girl to stand up,
Whenever her younger sibling shouts,

"MAMA!"

Suitcases

To immigrate is simply more than leaving home
behind.
It is to pack up everything you know,
And try to make it fit,
In places it never knew how to.

Burdens

A mother carries many burdens,
The burdens of her children, of her family, and her own.
Yet what makes her powerful,
What truly defines her strength,
Is her ability to carry the weight of all those burdens,
And still relentlessly fight for her family.

Culture

Our cultures are not limited to one environment,
They have the power to grow in unusual places,
Take forms in different people and spaces,
Sprouting however and wherever they please.
It is up to us whether they will flourish.

Alone

How is it possible,
To live on a such a ginormous planet,
Filled with billions of people,
But feel like you are fighting all your battles,

Alone.

“Where are you from?”

Nothing can truly explain the confusion felt,
When asked the question,
“Where are you from?”
Because you are then faced with the decision,
Between where you have been and where you
are,
And having to identify which one is home.

Mourning

The feeling that arises in my chest,
At any mention of home,
Can only be described as mournful.
I mourn where I grew up,
The ties with family and friends that have been severed.
I mourn the feeling of belonging that I used to wear with pride,
And I mourn my sense of self,
That has been lost in the abyss.

Stitches

How I wish I could stitch and sew all the parts of
my culture into a blanket,
Of all the delicacies, people, music, and dances,
So that on the days when I feel lost,
And my identity becomes a cold memory,
I can wrap all its fibres and fluffs around me,
Unifying myself with the familiarity of home
once again.

Contentment

What is contentment,
If not, the glow that consoles one's heart,
At the prospect of knowing,
That the tortures of their everyday toil,
Continues to illuminate the feasibility,
Of a brighter tomorrow.

Taste of Home

Each evening, the children wait patiently for
their mother to return home.
As she arrives, their eyes fixate on her routine.
She slips off her worn-out heels,
Then places her stack of resumes on the dining
table.
The deep lines etched on her face,
And the absence of her usual smile,
Cause unspoken questions to float through their
little minds.

But as she grabs her dotted apron,
Its scratchy material clinging to her chest,
The lines begin to fade, and a smile decorates
her face,
As she conducts an ensemble of pots and pans,
Creating a melodious tune of sizzling and
fizzling,
She relies on the only constant that reins comfort
each sorrowful night,
The taste of home.

Yearning

The young boy tries not to question his parents,
On why their two-bedroom townhouse,
Lacks the glamour of the mansion in which they used to reside,
Why the bus took the place of their shiny Mercedes-Benz,
And why his classmates always deliver harsh teases to his accent,
Staring down at him with their nationalism worn on their sleeves,
A sense of superiority hinted in their gaze.

The boy does not badger his parents,
About the ache that taunts his heart,
As he restlessly lays awake at night,
Tormented by the yearning for home.

True Strength

Sometimes a genuine display of strength,
Does not mean to be decked from head to toe
with armour,
Its silver sheen and hard shell,
Preparing you for the hardships to come,
Depicting the absolute absence of fear.
Sometimes true strength,
Is to allow yourself to show weakness and fear,
Yet still possess the courage to face it all.

Piece by Piece

Those who came before us have carefully laid a foundation,
For future generations to swim in pools of prosperity.
Years of work have led up to the reign of our parents,
Whose teachings and beliefs,
Have been weaved delicately into our intellect,
Bestowing upon us the responsibility,
To continue building that foundation,
Piece by piece.

Lines

How I miss the days,
When struggling to colour within the lines,
Was the hardest challenge I had to endure,
When the desire for validation was non-existent.
Now I colour inside the black barriers,
Afraid to venture beyond the protection they bring,
And discover a world,
That is unaccepting of who I am.

Loneliness

Loneliness is the enemy that acts as your friend,
While slowly enclosing itself around you,
Banishing you into a trap of your own creation.
The most damning part of all,
Is that this trap is not ceaseless,
But the will to escape it,
Is absent.

Lenses

I remember watching the world through
picturesque lenses,
Each colour appearing brighter every day,
Gifting me with delicate kisses of life.
Now, those lenses have darkened,
Fractures and cracks staining their former
smoothness,
Imperfection clouding their vision,
Life's vibrant kiss faded away,
And monotony materialized in its place instead.

The World is a Parent

Many believe that the role of a parent lies upon two people,
Who mold and shape their kin into who they are,
But the world is a parent as well.
It introduces people into our lives,
Who affect our fragile state of minds.
It presents us with opportunities,
To reap the fruits of our struggles,
And teaches us to be fit for survival.
The world cradles us just as our parents do,
Its grasp merely feels fainter.

The Back of My Mind

In the back of my mind,
The reminiscence of home resides.
The softness of my bed,
Its plush material comforting my aching back at night,
And lulling me to a peaceful sleep.
The smell of mahogany wood permeating the house,
Subtly entering my nose upon arrival from school each day.
The bubbly laughter that erupted throughout the whole house,
Whenever my boisterous cousins would visit.
But I cannot stay in the depths of my mind any longer,
Because life will continue to move in its steady pace,
While I struggle to find my own.

Self-Portrait

With the genesis of a new life comes a blank canvas,
Waiting to be caressed with the strokes of life,
Possessing a variety of glossy hues,
Composed of a rich mixture of culture, beliefs and traditions,
Uniting to fashion the self-portrait,
Of a unique soul.

Memories

Some of the most treasured moments in life are
the ones we don't remember,
Whether favourable or sorrowful,
Whether we laughed to a point where we
couldn't breathe,
Or cried so hard we couldn't see.
The moments of awe or disarray,
Or the moments that we wanted to skip through
and never relive.

Stories live within these forgotten memories.
Some we may not recall, while others may,
So that as we gaze towards what we thought we
once knew,
We can admire how time has gone by.
What once was present is now past,
Distant yet so close.

www.ingramcontent.com/pod-product-compliance
Lightning Source LLC
Chambersburg PA
CBHW051717130826
49812CB00034B/1228
* 9 7 8 9 3 5 7 2 1 2 1 5 1 *